Sunshine

Pupil's Book 4

Erarbeitet von
Stefanie Aschkar (Konstanz)
Tanja Beattie (Ebersberg)
Nadine Kerler (Ulm)
Caroline Schröder (München)
Maria Skejic (Frankfurt am Main)

Auf der Grundlage der Ausgabe von
Birgit Hollbrügge
und Ulrike Kraaz

Cornelsen

In deinem Buch findest du gelbe Notizzettel mit Symbolen:

Hier erfährst du
mehr über die
englische Sprache.

 Note

Hier erfährst du
mehr über
Großbritannien.

 Note

Hier sollst du
mehr zu einem
Thema herausfinden.

 Note

Symbols

 listen to your partner
or teacher

 read

 draw or write

 listen to the CD,
track 2

 talk

 play

⭐ extra

Contents

Welcome back **4**
days of the week, holidays, school subjects

1 A trip to London **6**
days of the week, food, sights and transport, the time

2 All year round **11**
months and days, numbers 13–45, seasons and weather

3 At the museum **16**
animals, body parts, directions

4 Keeping fit **21**
body and feelings, months and days, sports and hobbies

5 Emails from the USA **25**
family, jobs, New York, writing emails

6 A school play **30**
Looking back at Sunshine

Special days **35**
Bonfire Night, Christmas, Halloween

Looking at English **38**

Word list **40**

Welcome back

1 Talk about the picture. Say: *I can see ...*

2 Read the speech bubbles with a partner.

3 Talk about holidays. Ask a partner questions.

I was in the USA. Where were you?

OK.

Were you in Rome, Kate?

Yes. It was great!

How were your holidays, Emily?

I was at home.

Where was Samir?

He was in Germany.

Where were you in your holidays, Harry?

1 Talk about Emily's timetable. Say: *On Monday, Emily has Maths, ...*

2 Listen. What day is it?

> After lunch, I have...

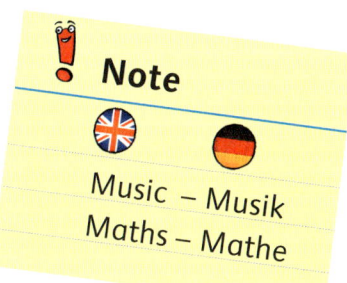

Science

Music

German

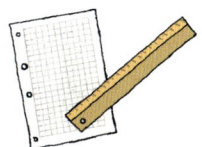
Maths

Time	Monday	Tuesday	Wednesday	Thursday	Friday
9.00 - 9.30	ASSEMBLY				
9.30 - 10.30	Maths	Maths	English	Music	Maths
10.30 - 10.45	PLAY				
10.45 - 11.45	English	German	Maths	Maths	English
11.45 - 1.00	LUNCH				
1.00 - 1.15	QUIET				
1.15 - 2.15	Music	Computers	Science	English	Art
2.15 - 3.15	German	P.E.	P.E.	Art	Computers

P.E. (Physical Education)

English

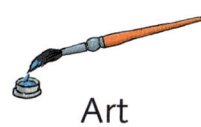
Art

Computers

1 A trip to London

🗨 **1** Talk about the map. What can you see?

📖 **2** Read the texts. Find the sights on the map.
Say: *Number 1 is…*

① **Tower Bridge** is a very famous bridge. It can open to let big ships through. It takes about 90 seconds to open.

② **London Zoo** is one of the oldest zoos in the world. You can see about 750 different kinds of animals there.

③ **Buckingham Palace** is the Queen's London home. On top of Buckingham Palace you can see the Union flag.

④ **Big Ben** is the name of a bell. The bell is inside the clock tower of Westminster Palace.

🇬🇧 **Note**

The London underground is called the "Tube".

3 Look at the map.
Listen and find the way.

⭐ Say where and when they go.
How do they get there?

🔍 **Note**

Find out more about the sights 7 and 8.

⑤ The **London Eye** is the biggest observation wheel in the world. It is 135 metres high.

⑥ **Madame Tussauds** is a famous wax museum. You can see film stars, sports stars, pop stars and the Royal Family there. Who is your favourite star?

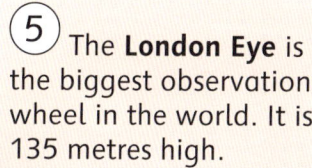

Let's talk

4 Read the dialogue. Talk to a partner.

⭐ More: Make up your own dialogue.

Route 274

Not Transferable

Fare: **Single £2.00**

Retain Ticket for Inspection

 1 Look at the pictures. Talk about the pictures.

 **2** Read the postcards. Say the numbers.

⭐ When was Harry's birthday?
What's the name of Harry's grandma?

 Note

Look at Kate's SMS.
What does she write?

LONDON EYE

Hello Jack,

I'm in London with Kate and her dad.
It's super! Thursday was my birthday.
We went on a boat trip on the River
Thames to the London Eye. It was
great. I could see Buckingham Palace
from the top of the London Eye.

Harry

Dear Grandma,

How are you? I'm in London with my
friend Kate and her dad.
It's Tuesday. London is great.
I like sitting at the top of the
red buses. Here's a picture of
Big Ben. Big Ben is a bell inside the
clock tower!

I hope you come to my
birthday party on Sunday.

Love, Harry

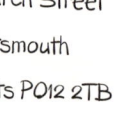

Mrs Benson

5 Birch Street

Portsmouth

Hants PO12 2TB

Hi Mum, Lndn is
gr8! 2day we are
going to Tower
Bridge. CU next
Mon.
Kate X

Dear Mum,

I like London. It's great!
Yesterday it was Harry's birthday.
Today we went to Hyde Park to eat
some ice cream and to play football.
We walked over Tower Bridge, too.
What a big bridge! You must go and
see Tower Bridge. It opens in the
middle. See you on Saturday.

Love, Kate

Mrs William

12 Morgan Street

Band

Story: **The Earl of Sandwich**

1 Listen to the story.

2 Read the dialogue.

3 Act it out.

Note

Who was the Earl of Sandwich? Find out more!

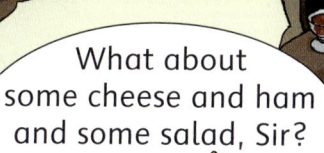

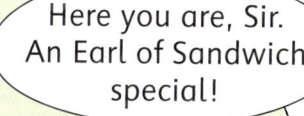

More to explore: **The Royal Family**

1 Listen. Point to the pictures.

2 Read the sentences.

> **Note**
>
> In which other countries are there still kings or queens? Find out!

People in Britain love the Royal Family.

Royal guards in front of Buckingham Palace.

The Royals are everywhere.

3 Read the sentences. Find the right pictures.

⭐ Talk about activities and times. Say: *At 10 a.m., William ...*

One day in the life of two Royals.

> **Note**
>
> a.m. = in the morning
> p.m. = in the afternoon

08:00 a.m.	Kate takes her dog for a walk.
10:00 a.m.	William visits a football team.
12:00	Kate and William have lunch.
02:00 p.m.	Kate visits pupils at a London school.
07:30 p.m.	Kate and William are at a concert.

1 What's the weather like? Say: *In picture 1, it's snowy …*

2 Read the sentences. Talk about the pictures.

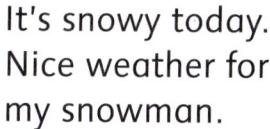

It's snowy today.
Nice weather for
my snowman.

It's foggy in London.

> **! Note**
>
> sun – sunny
> wind – windy

What a windy day!

It's sunny.

What a rainy day!

Look, it's very cloudy today.
It's going to rain.

What's
the weather
like today?

2

Let's talk

1 Read the dialogue. Talk to a partner.
⭐ More: Make up your own dialogue.

Hi, how are you?

I'm OK.

What's the weather like in London?

It's great, 20 degrees and sunny.

2 Look at the pictures. Talk to a partner. Say: *In Rome it's …*

Rome (15°C)

New York (3°C)

SUNDAY
MANCHESTER
32°C
Feels like: 32°C
Humidity: 63%
Pressure: 1012.1 MB
Wind: 23 KM/H
Sunrise: 5:52 AM
Sunset: 8:12 PM

MONDAY		29°C
TUESDAY		25°C
WEDNESDAY		23°C
THURSDAY		26°C

Paris (25°C)

Ankara (33°C)

London (13°C)

1 Read and match.

> Hi, I'm Robin. My birthday is in September, in autumn. In autumn, the leaves turn red and yellow. When it is windy, I like flying my kite. Do you like my birthday cake?

> My birthday is in spring.

> Hello, my name is Oona. I was born in summer, in July. When it is sunny and hot, I like eating ice cream. What do you do in summer?

> Hi, I'm Arian. My birthday is in April, in spring. In spring, there are lots of flowers. I like looking for Easter eggs. Do you like my tree?

> Hello, my name is Mathilda. My birthday is in winter, in February. Sometimes it is cold and snowy on my birthday. I like playing in the snow. Do you like my snowman?

2 Answer the questions.

- When is Robin's / Arian's / … birthday? Say: *Robin's birthday is in …*
- What's the weather like in spring / summer / …? Say: *In spring, it's …*
- What do the children like? Say: *Robin likes …*
- What about you? Say: *My birthday is in …*

1 Read the texts. Play the game.

	1 Go forward 2.	2 It's a snowy Saturday in January.	3	4	5 Snowdrops in winter.	6
START						
7 A birthday in March.	8	9 Daffodils in spring.	10	11 25° on Sunday.	12 A rainy Monday in June.	13 Go back 3.
14 A cold Tuesday in summer.	15	16 Throw again.	17 Red roses in July.	18	19	20 A sunny Wednesday in August.
21	22 A cloudy Friday in September.	23 A windy Thursday in October.	24 Spiders in autumn.	25	26 Miss a turn.	27 A foggy Monday in November.
28	29 15° on Christmas Day.	30	FINISH			

A snowy Saturday in January.	Go back 1.		Red roses in July.	Throw again.
Snowdrops in winter.	Go forward 1.		A sunny Wednesday in August.	Go forward 1.
A birthday in March.	Go forward 3.		A cloudy Friday in September.	Miss a turn.
Daffodils in spring.	Go forward 2.		A windy Thursday in October.	Go back 2.
25° on Sunday.	Throw again.		Spiders in autumn.	Go forward 2.
A rainy Monday in June.	Go back 2.		A foggy Monday in November.	Miss a turn.
A cold Tuesday in summer.	Miss a turn.		15° on Christmas Day.	Go back 3.

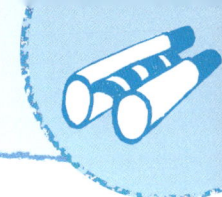

1 Talk about the pictures.
When is the wind helpful? When is the wind dangerous?

1 2 3

4 5 6

2 Read the rhyme.

⭐ Say the rhyme.

> The kites go up, the kites go down.
> See how they fly all over the town.
> The children run and jump and play,
> Because they love a windy day.

You need:

a glass bottle

a candle

matches

3 Do the experiment with your teacher.

1. Put the candle behind the bottle.

Watch the film.

2. Blow hard on the bottle. What happens to the candle?

→ 🔘 1
DVD

1 What animals are in the museum? Say: *There's …*

2 Read the speech bubbles. Talk to a partner.

29 crocodiles

18 dinosaurs

I like the crocodiles.

What animals do you want to see?

I want to see the whales. What about you?

This is the Natural History Museum in London.

There's a mole in the museum.

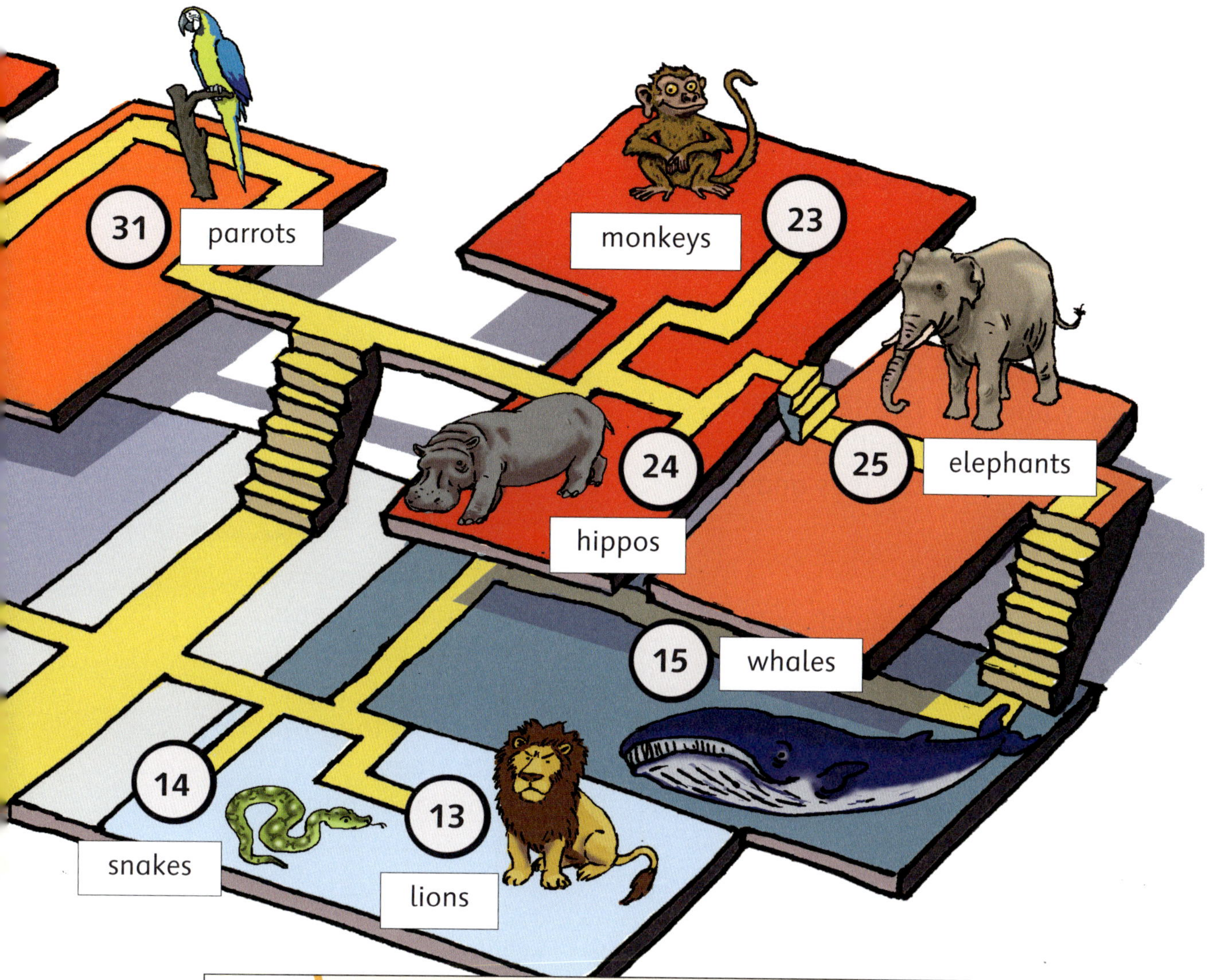

31 parrots

23 monkeys

24 hippos

25 elephants

15 whales

14 snakes

13 lions

Let's talk

3 Read the dialogue. Talk to a partner.
⭐ More: Make your own dialogue.

Excuse me, please. Where are the whales?

They are downstairs, in room 15.

Go straight, then turn left.

 **1** Read the texts. Which animal is it?

Think of one more animal.
Talk, draw or show.

They live in the jungle.
They eat leaves and grass.
They have got big ears.
They have got two long teeth.
They have got small eyes.
They have got big legs and feet.

They live underground.
They eat snails and worms.
They have got small eyes,
a short tail and
black fur.
They are blind.

They have got small ears.
They have got long arms.
They have got two legs.
They have got a long tail.
They live in trees.
They eat bananas and leaves.

2 Read the presentation rules.

 Make notes.

 Know your text.

 Speak loudly.

 Look at the class.

 Show pictures.

I want to talk about crocodiles. Crocodiles are wild animals …

Story: **Harry's night at the museum**

1 Talk about the pictures.

2 Read the speech bubbles.

⭐ Complete the speech bubbles.
Work with a partner.

More to explore: **The Jurassic Coast**

 **1** Listen. Point to the pictures.

 2 Read the texts.

 **Note**

What was the biggest, smallest, fastest, heaviest, longest dinosaur?
Find out!

1

Jurassic Coast

The Jurassic Coast is a region in South England.

2

dinosaur fossil

3

dinosaur footprint

4

ammonites

5

a fish

6

dinosaur museum

At the dinosaur museum in Dorchester you can learn a lot about dinosaurs.

Watch the film.

1 Read the posters. Name the club.

2 Work with a partner. Talk about the clubs.

3 Listen. What club do the children want to go to?

Where's the dance club?

It's in …

When's the … club?

It's on …

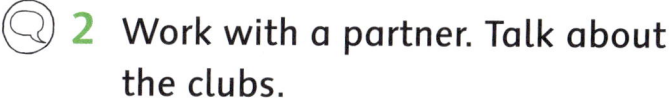

Girls' football club
Girls <u>can</u> play football!

When: Wednesday
Where: In the park

Do you like computers?
Then come to the

Computer club

When: Wednesday
Where: Computer room

Do you like computers?

Dance to your favourite songs at the

Dance club

When: Thursday
Where: Room 12

Move your body at the

Fit kids club

When: Friday
Where: High Street Fitness club

Dog? Cat? Guinea pig?
What is your favourite animal?

Pet club

When: Tuesday
Where: Room 6a

Judo club
Do judo with your friends.

When: Monday
Where: Room 4

 1 Listen. What can Linda do?

 2 Read the dialogue with a partner.

 Make up your own dialogue.

Hi, **Linda**. Can I ask you some questions about sport?

Yes, OK.

What's your favourite sport?

My favourite sport is **skiing**.

What about tennis? Can you **play tennis**?

No, I can't play tennis. But I can **play table tennis**.

Do you go to the **table tennis club on Tuesday**?

No, I go to the computer club **on Tuesday**.

Thanks for the interview. Bye!

You're welcome. Bye!

Story: **Giraffes can't dance**

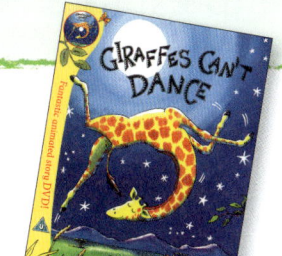

1 Listen. Point to the pictures.

2 Read the story.

Gerald the giraffe likes dancing. But when he dances, his legs get in the way and he falls down.

The other animals laugh at Gerald when he dances. They shout out: 'Giraffes can't dance!' Poor Gerald! He leaves the dance floor. He feels sad and lonely.

A cricket sees Gerald and says: 'Don't be sad. You can dance! Everyone can dance. Just listen to the music around you!'

Gerald listens to the music. His legs start to move and then his neck starts to sway. Gerald is so excited. 'I can dance. I can dance.' He feels wonderful.

The other animals see Gerald dancing. They start to clap. 'Wow, Gerald, you are a really good dancer!' they say. Gerald is so proud that he can dance. 'Thank you, thank you!' he says. Now all the animals are his friends. He feels very happy.

1 Listen and point to the pictures.

①  ②  ③  ④

2 Look at the pictures. Read the rules. Talk to a partner about the rules.

🇬🇧 **Note**

Viele englische Kinder spielen Rounders auf dem Schulhof. Kennst du ein ähnliches Spiel?

You need:

a bat	a ball	4 posts	6-15 players

① Form two teams.

batting team   fielding team

② Choose a bowler.

bowler

③ The bowler bowls the ball. The batter hits the ball.

④ The batter runs from post to post.

Watch the film.

The team with the most rounders wins.

→ DVD 4

1 Talk about the picture.
What are the friends doing?

Kate, Great Britain

Leon, Germany

Matt, USA

Note

Dein Name, deine Adresse, deine Telefonnummer oder dein Geburtsdatum gehen nicht jeden etwas an. Sprich immer zuerst mit deiner Lehrerin, deinem Lehrer oder deinen Eltern, bevor du im Internet von dir erzählst.

STOP

2 Read the questions.

3 Answer the questions.

What's your password? ●●●●●●●●●●●●

What's your name? *Kate*

How old are you? *I'm 10 years old.*

When's your birthday? *In May.*

Where are you from? *I'm from Great Britain.*

What's your nickname? *Kitty*

What are your hobbies? *dancing, swimming*

My password is top secret!

 1 **Talk about the pictures.**

①
Statue of Liberty

②
Empire State Building

③
Central Park

④
Brooklyn Bridge

⑤
yellow cab

 2 **Listen to Matt's rap. Point to the pictures.**

3 **Read the text.**

⭐ **Do the rap.**

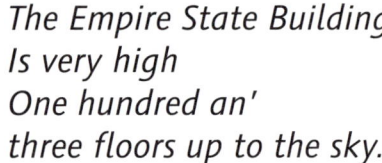

Welcome to New York
Welcome to the sights
Welcome to the city
That never sleeps at nights.

Go to Central Park
Have a picnic in the sun
Skate, skate, play or walk
Have lots of fun.

New York City is the place 2 B. Yo!
New York City is the place 4 me.

The Empire State Building
Is very high
One hundred an'
three floors up to the sky.

Over Brooklyn Bridge
You can bike, walk or ride
Or take a yellow cab
From side to side.

One more sight
You have to see
And that's the famous
Statue of Liberty.

 1 Read Kate's email. What does she write about?

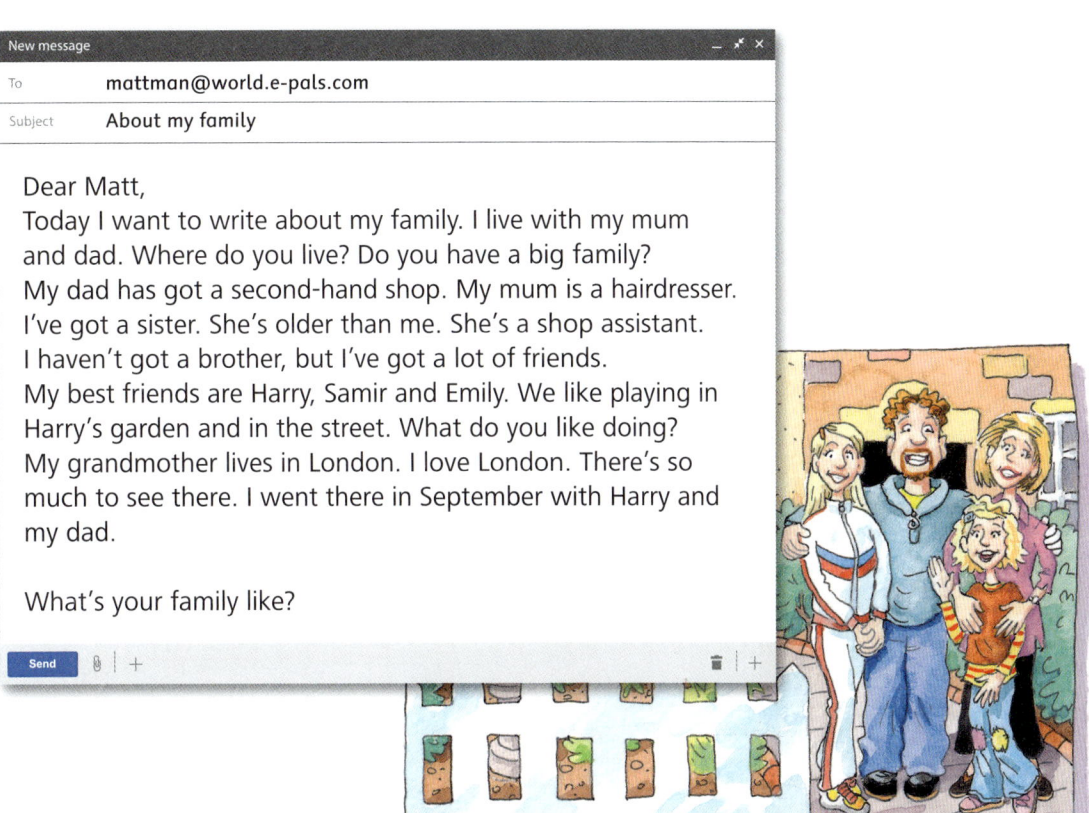

New message   _ ⤢ ×

| To | mattman@world.e-pals.com |
| Subject | About my family |

Dear Matt,
Today I want to write about my family. I live with my mum
and dad. Where do you live? Do you have a big family?
My dad has got a second-hand shop. My mum is a hairdresser.
I've got a sister. She's older than me. She's a shop assistant.
I haven't got a brother, but I've got a lot of friends.
My best friends are Harry, Samir and Emily. We like playing in
Harry's garden and in the street. What do you like doing?
My grandmother lives in London. I love London. There's so
much to see there. I went there in September with Harry and
my dad.

What's your family like?

Send   🖉

 2 Listen to Matt's email.

 3 Read the text.

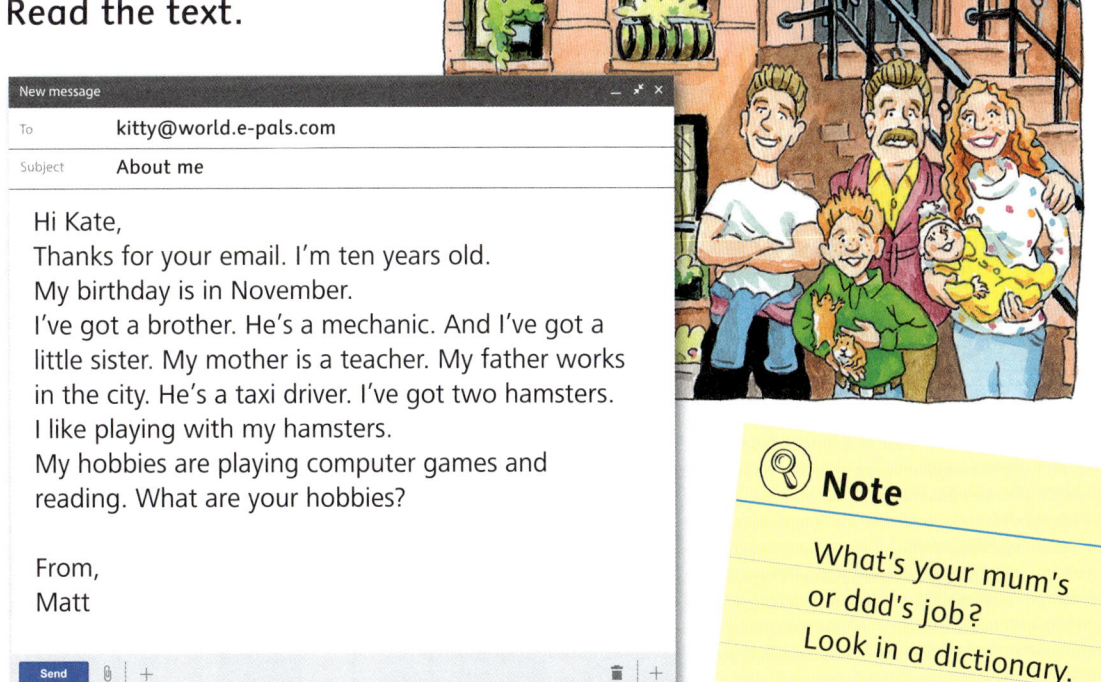

New message   _ ⤢ ×

| To | kitty@world.e-pals.com |
| Subject | About me |

Hi Kate,
Thanks for your email. I'm ten years old.
My birthday is in November.
I've got a brother. He's a mechanic. And I've got a
little sister. My mother is a teacher. My father works
in the city. He's a taxi driver. I've got two hamsters.
I like playing with my hamsters.
My hobbies are playing computer games and
reading. What are your hobbies?

From,
Matt

Send   🖉

Note

What's your mum's
or dad's job?
Look in a dictionary.

Story: **A day in New York**

1 Talk about the pictures.

2 Read the text.

On the bus, please.

Great!

Off we go.

Here's the Brooklyn Bridge.

Oh, what a great bridge.

I wish I was a taxi driver in New York.

On the bus, please.

Oh, what a great building.

Here's the Empire State Building.

I wish I was a shop assistant in New York.

FUN FASHIONS

Oh, what a great statue.

I wish I was a mechanic in New York.

17? Oh no! Where are Andy, Emma and Justin?

I wish I was a police officer in New York.

I wish I was at home.

5

 1 Read the texts about John, the police officer.

 2 Listen to your partner. Point to the right picture.

Hello, my name is John.
I'm a police officer
in New York City.

In the city
we patrol by car.

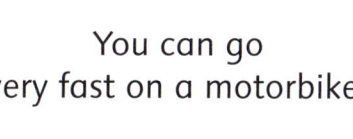

You can go
very fast on a motorbike.

In Central Park
we use horses.

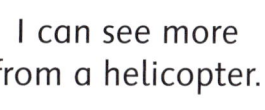

I can see more
from a helicopter.

Do you like my badge?

3 Listen. Talk to a partner.

⭐ More: Make up your own dialogue.

Do you want police, fire or ambulance?

What's your name?

What's your address?

Where are you?

OK. Stay where you are.

Ambulance. My brother needs help.

My name is Mark.

32 Green Street.

I'm at the Empire State Building.

OK.

Story: **The school inspector**

1 Read the story.

1
Good morning, Mrs Brown.

Sorry, I'm late.

Yes, you are, Simon. Sit down.

2
Have you got your pencils?

Yes, we have.

Give it back, Jack!

3
What a bad class you are.

That isn't right, inspector. They're good pupils.

4
Do you know about animals?

Of course, we do.

crocodile

Crocodiles are wild animals.

That isn't right. They're good pupils.

5
That was bad.

6

Do you know a rhyme?

Of course, we do!

I can say: The elephant goes like this and that.

7

I'm very angry. What a bad class.

8

Can you read?

Of course, we can!

I know a story about the Earl of Sandwich.

9

That was bad!

No, that isn't right, inspector.

10

I'm not the school inspector. Sorry, Mrs Brown.

He's the caretaker!

He isn't the school inspector.

11

What a nice class, Mrs Brown!

Thank you, Ms Honey. They're good pupils.

 1 What did you learn?
What can you say in English?
Read the texts.

 2 Talk about the units.

I know the colours and numbers in English.

I can talk about my family and friends.

How did

I can say which pets I like.

That was OK.

I can talk about my school things.

That was not so good.

That was great!

I can talk about clothes.

I can talk about rooms and furniture.

I can buy food and drinks.

I can read a story book.

I can say what time it is.

I can talk about the weather, seasons and my birthday month.

ou like it?

I like …

I don't like … because …

My favourite words are …

I was good at …

I want to learn more about …

I can do a presentation about animals.

Know your text.

Speak loudly.

Look at the clas

Show pictures.

Crocodiles are wild animals …

I can say what my hobbies are.

I can read the story about Gerald the giraffe.

I can write about myself and my family.

kitty@world.e-pals.com

About me

Hi Kate,
Thanks for your email. I'm ten years old.
My birthday is in November.
I've got a brother. He's a mechanic. And I've got a little sister. My mother is a teacher. My father works in the city. He's a taxi driver. I've got two hamsters.
I like playing with my hamsters.
My hobbies are playing computer games and reading. What are your hobbies?

From,
Matt

Send

I know about Halloween.

1 **Read the rhyme, the chant and the rap.**

Do you know a rhyme?

Of course, I do!

The elephant

The elephant goes
Like this, like that.
He's terribly big,
And he's terribly fat.
He has no fingers,
He has big toes,
And goodness gracious,
What a nose!

Holidays

I was in London,
She was in Rome,
He was in Ankara,
And where were you?
I was at home.

London

Rome

Ankara

Matt's rap

Welcome to New York
Welcome to the sights
Welcome to the city
That never sleeps at nights.

Go to Central Park
Have a picnic in the sun
Skate, skate, play or walk
Have lots of fun.

New York City is the place 2 B. Yo!
New York City is the place 4 me.

1 Talk about the picture.

How many ghosts, monsters, pumpkins, skeletons, … can you see?

2 Listen to the rhyme.

3 Read the rhyme.

Trick or treat,
Listen to the beat.
We want only
Sweets to eat.

Trick or treat,
Smell my feet.
Give me something
Good to eat!

Special days: **Bonfire Night**

1. Talk about the pictures.
2. Listen to the rhyme.
3. Read the rhyme.
⭐ Say the rhyme.

Remember, remember
The fifth of November,
Gunpowder, treason and plot.
I see no reason
Why gunpowder treason
Should ever be forgot.

1

Penny for the Guy.

2

3

4

 1 Listen to the story. Point to the pictures.

 2 Read the story.

 ⭐ Sing the song. Find the matching pictures.

Rudolph is a reindeer. He has a red and shiny nose.

The other reindeer laugh at Rudolph's nose.

Poor Rudolph is sad and lonely.

It's Christmas Eve. It's very foggy. Santa asks Rudolph for help.

Rudolph helps Santa. He guides the sleigh. He shows the reindeer the way.

Rudolph is very proud and very happy. The reindeer are his friends. They all love him. Rudolph is never sad and lonely again.

Looking at English

So verändern sich die Wörter in der Mehrzahl:
Wenn du von mehreren Dingen sprichst, hängst du ein ‚s' an.

one book – two book**s**
one apple – two apple**s**

➜ Es gibt Ausnahmen, die du dir merken musst:

one child- two child**ren**
one hobb**y** – two hobb**ies**

So sagst du, dass jemanden etwas gehört:

This is Tim**'s** book.   This is Anne**'s** pencil case.

🔍 **Note**

Finde Beispiele in deinem Pupil's Book!

Diese Wörter brauchst du, um Fragen zu stellen:

What? = Was?
What is this?

When? = Wann?
When is your birthday?

Where? = Wo?
Where is my book?

Who? = Wer?
Who is on the phone?

How? = Wie?
How are you?

How many? = Wie viele?
How many children like chocolate?

How much? = Wie viel?
How much is the orange juice?

➜ Es gibt Ausnahmen, die du dir merken musst:

How much is …?   = Was kostet …?
What time is it?   = Wie spät ist es?
What's your name? = Wie heißt du?

So fangen viele Fragen an:

Do you like …?   = Magst du …?
Can I have …?   = Kann ich … haben?
Have you got …?   = Hast du …?
Are you happy/sad/angry? = Bist du glücklich, traurig, wütend?

Looking at English

So kannst du über dich und andere sprechen:

I am   you are   he is   she is

it is   we are   you are   they are

Manche Wörter werden abgekürzt:

I am = I'm
you are = you're
he is = he's
she is = she's
it is = it's
we are = we're
you are = you're
they are = they're

I'm

I can = I can't
where is = where's
what is = what's
I would like = I'd like
I have got = I've got

🔍 **Note**

Finde Beispiele in deinem Pupil's Book!

Manche Wörter haben mehrere Bedeutungen:

you   =   du, ihr

it   =   er, sie, es

Word list

A

about über
again noch einmal, wieder
angry verärgert
animal Tier
answer antworten, Lösung
Art Kunst (Schulfach)
ask fragen
at bei, im, um
autumn Herbst

B

back Rücken
bad schlecht
ballet Ballett
basketball Basketball
be sein
because weil
behind hinter
belly Bauch
bend beugen
big groß
birthday Geburtstag
blackboard Tafel
blow out auspusten
boat Boot
bonfire Lagerfeuer
book Buch
boy Junge
bread Brot
brother Bruder
bus Bus
bus driver Busfahrer/in
bush Busch
but aber
butter Butter
buy kaufen

C

calendar Kalender
camel Kamel
can können
candle Kerze
car Auto
caretaker Hausmeister
chair Stuhl
cent (hier: amerikanischer) Cent
cheese Käse
chicken Huhn

chips Pommes frites
chocolate Schokolade
Christmas Weihnachten
city Großstadt
clap klatschen
class Klasse
classroom Klassenraum
clock Uhr
clock tower Glockenturm
cloudy wolkig
club AG, Klub, Verein
colour Farbe, ausmalen
come kommen
Computers Computer (Schulfach)
crocodile Krokodil
cut out ausschneiden

D

daffodil Osterglocke
dance tanzen
dangerous gefährlich
day Tag
Dear ... Liebe/r ...
degree(s) Grad
dinosaur Dinosaurier
do machen, tun
do ballet Ballett tanzen
do judo Judo betreiben
dollar ($) (hier: amerikanischer) Dollar
door Tür
downstairs unten
draw zeichnen
dream Traum
drink trinken, Getränk
driver Fahrer

E

ear Ohr
eat essen
egg Ei
elephant Elefant
email E-Mail
England England
English englisch, Englisch (Schulfach)
e-pal E-Mail-Freund/in
euro (€) Euro
evening Abend
eye Auge

Word list

F

famous berühmt
father Vater
Father Christmas Weihnachtsmann
favourite Lieblings-
feed füttern
fireworks Feuerwerk
flag Flagge
flap auf und ab bewegen
fly fliegen
foggy neblig
food Essen
foot, feet Fuß, Füße
football Fußball
forget vergessen
forward vorwärts
Friday Freitag
from aus, von

G

game Spiel
German deutsch, Deutsch (Schulfach)
Germany Deutschland
ghost Geist
giraffe Giraffe
girl Mädchen
give geben
glue kleben
go gehen
Good luck! Viel Glück!
Goodness gracious! Du meine Güte!
grandfather, grandpa Großvater, Opa
grandmother, grandma Großmutter, Oma
Great Britain Großbritannien
gunpowder Schießpulver

H

hairdresser Friseur/in
half past halb (Uhrzeit)
Halloween Halloween
ham Schinken
happen geschehen
happy glücklich
have (got) haben
have to müssen
he er
head Kopf
hello hallo
help helfen, Hilfe

helpful hilfreich
her ihr/ihre
here hier
hippo Nilpferd
his sein/seine
hobby Hobby
holidays Ferien
(at) home zu Hause
hop hopsen, springen
hope hoffen
horse Pferd
hot heiß, warm
house Haus
how wie
how many wie viele
how much wie viel

I

idea Idee
ill krank
in in
in front of vor
inspector Inspektor/in, Schulrat/-rätin
is ist
it es

J

job Beruf, Job
judo Judo
jump springen
jungle Dschungel

K

king König
kite Drachen
knee Knie
know kennen, wissen

L

late spät
leaf, leaves Blatt, Blätter
left links
leg Bein
lesson Schulstunde
Let's go! Los!
lettuce Kopfsalat
line Linie, Reihe
lion Löwe
listening to music Musik hören
little klein

live leben, wohnen
long lang
look at betrachten
loud, loudly laut
love lieben
Love, ... Liebe Grüße ...

M

make machen
many viel/e
matches Streichhölzer
Maths Mathe (Schulfach)
mechanic Mechaniker/in
meeting friends Freunde treffen
miss a turn aussetzen
Monday Montag
monkey Affe
morning Morgen
mother Mutter
motorbike Motorrad
move (sich) bewegen
much viel
museum Museum
Music Musik (Schulfach)
my mein/e

N

name Name
next to neben
nice nett
nickname Spitzname
nose Nase
not nicht
notes Noten, Notizen
number Nummer

O

o'clock ...Uhr
of course natürlich
old alt
on auf
open offen/öffnen

P

P.E. (= Physical Education)
Sport (Schulfach)
paper Papier
parrot Papagei
password Passwort
photo Foto
picture Bild

plane Flugzeug
play spielen, Theaterspiel
please bitte
plot Verschwörung
point to auf ... zeigen
police officer Polizist/in
police station Polizeiwache
postcard Postkarte
present Geschenk
pumpkin Kürbis
pupil Schüler/in
put legen, stellen

Q

quarter past/to viertel nach/vor
(Uhrzeit)
queen Königin
quiet leise

R

rainy regnerisch
read lesen
remember erinnern
rhyme Reim
ride a horse reiten
right rechts
river Fluss
rose Rose
run laufen

S

sad traurig
salad (zubereiteter) Salat
Santa, Santa Claus
Weihnachtsmann (in den USA)
Saturday Samstag
savannah Savanne
say sagen
scared verängstigt
Science Sachunterricht (Schulfach)
sea Meer
season Jahreszeit
see sehen
she sie
shop assistant Verkäufer/in
short kurz
shoulder Schulter
show zeigen
sight Sehenswürdigkeit
sing singen

sister Schwester
sit sitzen
skeleton Skelett
ski Ski, Ski fahren
small klein
snake Schlange
snap schnipsen
snowdrop Schneeglöckchen
snowy verschneit
speak sprechen
spider Spinne
sports Sportarten
spring Frühling
stamp aufstampfen
star Star
street Straße
stretch dehnen, strecken
strong stark
subject Fach, Schulfach
summer Sommer
Sunday Sonntag
sunny sonnig
sweets Süßigkeiten
swim schwimmen

T

table Tisch
table tennis Tischtennis
tail Schwanz
talk reden
taxi Taxi
taxi driver Taxifahrer/in
tea Tee
teacher Lehrer/in
temperature Temperatur
tennis Tennis
text message, SMS SMS
there dort
they sie
this diese/r/s
throw werfen
Thursday Donnerstag
ticket Fahrkarte
tiger Tiger
time Zeit
timetable Stundenplan
to nach, zu
today heute
toe Zeh
toilet Toilette

tomato/es Tomate/n
tooth, teeth Zahn, Zähne
touch anfassen, berühren
train Zug
treason Verrat
tree Baum
Tuesday Dienstag
tummy Bauch
turn abbiegen
turn around umdrehen

U

under unter
underground U-Bahn
understand verstehen
upstairs oben
USA USA (= Vereinigte Staaten von
   Amerika)
useful nützlich

V

Vampire Vampir

W

walk gehen
want wollen
watching TV fernsehen
water Wasser
we wir
weather Wetter
weather report Wetterbericht
Wednesday Mittwoch
weekend Wochenende
welcome willkommen
whale Wal
what was
wheel Rad
when wann
where wo
who wer
why warum
wiggle hin und her bewegen, zappeln
wild wild
windy windig
winter Winter
wish wünschen
witch Hexe

Word list

A

abbiegen turn
Abend evening
Affe monkey
alt old
anfassen touch
anschauen look at
antworten answer
auf on
auf und ab bewegen flap
aufstampfen stamp
auf ... zeigen point to
Auge eye
aus from
ausmalen colour (in)
ausschneiden cut out
aussetzen miss a turn
Auto car

B

Ballett ballet
Ballett machen do ballet
Basketball basketball
Bauch belly, tummy
Baum tree
bei at
Bein leg
Beruf job
berühmt famous
berühren touch
beugen bend
(sich) bewegen move
Bild picture
bitte please
Blatt, Blätter leaf, leaves
Boot boat
Brot bread
Bruder brother
Buch book
Bus bus
Busch bush
Busfahrer/in bus driver
Butter butter

C

Cent cent
Computer (Schulfach) Computers

D

dehnen stretch
Deutsch (Schulfach), deutsch German

Deutschland Germany
Dienstag Tuesday
diese/r/s this
Dinosaurier dinosaur
Dollar ($) dollar
Donnerstag Thursday
dort there
Drachen kite
Dschungel jungle
Du meine Güte! Goodness gracious!

E

Ei egg
Elefant elephant
E-Mail email
E-Mail-Freund/in e-pal
England England
Englisch (Schulfach), englisch English
er he
erinnern remember
es it
essen eat
Essen food
Euro (€) euro

F

Fach, Schulfach subject
Fahrer driver
Fahrkarte ticket
Farbe colour
Ferien holidays
fernsehen watching TV
Feuerwerk fireworks
Flagge flag
fliegen fly
Flugzeug plane
Fluss river
Foto photo
fragen ask
Freitag Friday
Freunde treffen meeting friends
Friseur/in hairdresser
Frühling spring
Fuß, Füße foot, feet
Fußball football
füttern feed

G

geben give
gefährlich dangerous
gehen go, walk

Word list

Geist ghost
geschehen happen
Geschenk present
Getränk drink
Giraffe giraffe
Glockenturm clock tower
glücklich happy
Grad degree(s)
groß big
Großbritannien Great Britain
Großmutter grandmother
Großstadt city
Großvater grandfather

H
haben have (got)
halb (Uhrzeit) half past/to
hallo hello
Halloween Halloween
Haus house
Hausmeister caretaker
heiß hot
helfen help
Herbst autumn
heute today
Hexe witch
hier here
hin und her bewegen, zappeln wiggle
Hilfe help
hilfreich helpful
Hobby hobby
hoffen hope
hopsen hop
Huhn chicken

I
Idee idea
ihr, ihre her, its
in in
ist is

J
Jahreszeit season
Job job
Judo judo
Judo betreiben do judo

K
Kalender calendar
Kamel camel
Käse cheese

kaufen buy
kennen know
Klasse class
Klassenraum classroom
klatschen clap
kleben glue
Klebstift glue stick
Kleid dress
klein little, small
Klub, AG club
Knie knee
kommen come
König king
Königin queen
können can
Kopf head
Kopfsalat lettuce
krank ill
Krokodil crocodile
Kunst (Schulfach) Art
Kürbis pumpkin
kurz short

L
Lagerfeuer bonfire
lang long
laufen run
laut loud, loudly
leben, wohnen live
legen put
Lehrer/in teacher
leise quiet
lesen read
Liebe/r … Dear …
Liebe Grüße … Love, …
lieben love
Lieblings- favourite
Linie line
links left
Los! Let's go!
Löwe lion

M
machen do, make
Mathe (Schulfach) Maths
Mechaniker/in mechanic
Meer sea
mein/e my
Mittwoch Wednesday
Montag Monday

Morgen morning
Motorrad motorbike
Museum museum
Musik (Schulfach) Music
Musik hören listening to music
müssen have to
Mutter mother

N

nach, zu to
Name name
Nase nose
natürlich of course
neben next to
neblig foggy
nett nice
nicht not
Nilpferd hippo
noch einmal again
Noten, Notizen notes
Nummer number
nützlich useful

O

oben upstairs
offen open
Ohr ear
Oma grandma
Opa grandpa
Osterglocke daffodil

P

Papagei parrot
Papier paper
Passwort password
Pferd horse
Polizeiwache police station
Polizist/in police officer
Pommes frites chips
Postkarte postcard

R

Rad wheel
rechts right
reden talk
regnerisch rainy
Reihe line
Reim rhyme
reiten ride a horse
Rose rose
Rücken back

S

Sachunterricht (Schulfach) Science
sagen say
Salat (zubereitet) salad
Samstag Saturday
Savanne savannah
Schießpulver gunpowder
Schinken ham
Schlange snake
schlecht bad
Schneeglöckchen snowdrop
schnipsen snap
Schokolade chocolate
Schüler/in pupil
Schulfach (school) subject
Schulstunde lesson
Schulter shoulder
Schwanz tail
Schwester sister
schwimmen swim
sehen look, see
Sehenswürdigkeit sight
sein be
sein/e his
sein/e, ihr/e its
sie she, they
singen sing
sitzen sit
Skelett skeleton
Ski, Ski fahren ski
SMS SMS, text message
Sommer summer
sonnig sunny
Sonntag Sunday
spät late
Spiel game
spielen play
Spinne spider
Spitzname nickname
Sport (Schulfach) P.E. (= Physical Education)
Sportarten sports
sprechen speak
springen jump
Star star
stark strong
stellen put
Straße street
strecken stretch

Stuhl chair
Stundenplan timetable
Süßigkeiten sweets

T

Tafel blackboard
Tag day
tanzen dance
Taxi taxi
Taxifahrer/in taxi driver
Tee tea
Temperatur temperature
Tennis tennis
Theaterspiel play
Tier animal
Tiger tiger
Tisch table
Tischtennis table tennis
Toilette toilet
Tomate/n tomato/es
Traum dream
traurig sad
trinken drink
Tür door

U

U-Bahn underground
über about
Uhr clock, ... o'clock
um at
umdrehen turn around
unten downstairs
unter under
USA (Vereinigte Staaten von Amerika) USA

V

Vampir vampire
Vater father
verängstigt scared
verärgert angry
vergessen forget
Verkäufer/in shop assistant
Verrat treason
verschneit snowy
Verschwörung plot
verstehen understand
viel much
viel/e many
Viel Glück! Good luck!

viertel vor/nach (Uhrzeit) quarter to/past
von from
vor in front of
vorwärts forward

W

Wal whale
wann when
warm hot
warum why
was what
Wasser water
Weihnachten Christmas
Weihnachtsmann Father Christmas, Santa Claus (USA)
weil because
wer who
werfen throw
Wetter weather
Wetterbericht weather report
wie how
wie viel how much
wie viele how many
wild wild
willkommen welcome
windig windy
Winter winter
wir we
wissen know
wo where
Wochenende weekend
wohnen live
wolkig cloudy
wollen want
wünschen wish

Z

Zahn, Zähne tooth, teeth
Zeh toe
zeichnen draw
zeigen show
Zeit time
zu to
Zug train
zu Hause (at) home

Sunshine

Lehrwerk für den früh beginnenden Englischunterricht

Pupil's Book 4

Erarbeitet von
Stefanie Keller, Konstanz; Tanja Beattie, Ebersberg;
Nadine Kerler, Ulm; Caroline Schröder, München;
Maria Sussex, Frankfurt am Main

Auf der Grundlage der Ausgabe von
Birgit Hollbrügge, Bielefeld; Ulrike Kraaz, Werther

Beratende Mitwirkung
Uwe Becker, Mannheim; Margit Butscher-Wich,
Bad Abbach; Michael Duscha, Braunschweig;
Renate Hafner, Blaustein; Siân Williams-Hahn,
Schorndorf (englischsprachige Texte)

Verlagsredaktion
Daniela Aue

Illustration
Beehive Illustration, Cirencester, England:
Mike Phillips, Neil Chapman; Volker Fredrich,
Hamburg; Mary Hall, Bath, England

Gesamtgestaltung
Corinna Babylon, Berlin

Technische Umsetzung
Michaela Müller für Corngreen GmbH, Leipzig

www.cornelsen.de

1. Auflage, 5. Druck 2024
Alle Drucke dieser Auflage sind inhaltlich unverändert
und können im Unterricht nebeneinander verwendet werden.

© 2015 Cornelsen Schulverlage GmbH, Berlin
© 2017 Cornelsen Verlag GmbH,
Mecklenburgische Str. 53, 14197 Berlin

Druck: Drukarnia Dimograf Sp. z o.o., Bielsko-Biała

ISBN 978-3-06-083765-6 (Schulbuch)
ISBN 978-3-06-081111-3 (E-Book)

PEFC-zertifiziert
Dieses Produkt
stammt aus
nachhaltig
bewirtschafteten
Wäldern und
kontrollierten Quellen
PEFC/32-31-076   www.pefc.pl